The Truth
of the
Gospel

A Study in Galatians

Alisa Weir

ISBN 979-8-89345-340-9 (paperback)
ISBN 979-8-89345-341-6 (digital)

Christian Faith Publishing
832 Park Avenue
Meadville, PA 16335
www.christianfaithpublishing.com

Printed in the United States of America

Contents

Whom shall he teach knowledge? and whom shall he make to understand doctrine? them that are weaned from the milk, and drawn from the breasts.

—Isaiah 28:9

Preface

Before we begin, I would like to talk about mindsets. We all probably have certain mindsets or beliefs, which guide our thinking and interpretations of things. People can have political mindsets or even religious ones. Sometimes it is hard to talk to someone that has a different mindset than our own. Mindsets can separate people into different political parties and into different religious denominations as well.

However, mindsets can be good if they are true. Of course, we all believe that our own beliefs are true or else we wouldn't believe them. On the other hand, mindsets can keep us from seeing other points of view or beliefs. What if something we believe is not true? If we are not open-minded enough to consider it, then we may be holding onto a belief that is not true, and we may even be deceived. God forbid, right?

Now, as a Christian, I believe that the Bible is true, that God is real, and that Jesus Christ came to save sinners. Most Christians probably believe those same things. However, there are many different denominations and lots of different doctrines or opinions about what the Bible says. Those doctrines can't all be right, or we would all agree with one another. What if something I have been taught is not true? Am I willing to consider it?

Somehow, early in my Christian walk, I was misled to think that the Sabbath is Sunday. A dear Christian friend and mentor once told me that I should not do any work on Sunday because, she said, it's the Lord's Day. So I assumed that meant that Sunday was the Sabbath. She had the right heart to honor the Lord, but she had the wrong day. I eventually learned that Saturday is really the Sabbath.

Anyway, as you can see, I started to put some mindsets into place, beliefs about the Bible that I picked up here and there, and mindsets about what we should or should not be doing as Christians. I remember the time I decided that I should stop going to garage sales on Sundays.

Then there was the time when a friend told me about a friend of hers who was talking about keeping the feasts of the Lord. I had read about the Lord's feasts in the Bible. There is the Feast of Passover and Feast of Trumpets and the Feast of Tabernacles for example. But when my friend told me about a Christian man that was talking about keeping the feasts, I thought in my mind, *Isn't that going backwards?* I mean, we Christians know we don't need to do those things anymore, or do we?

Anyway, after doing some online research, I learned how the Sabbath was eventually changed from Saturday to Sunday, at least in most churches. And now it has become like a doctrine that we should meet and worship on Sundays. Because I was hungry for answers, I searched online for years. And it seemed like I'd read through volumes of materials just to find one nugget of truth. But it wasn't until, finally, I prayed and said, "Lord, just lead me to your truth" that I was led to a certain website and then went to a meeting to hear from a Jewish prophet.

At the meetings, I learned about the *identity* of the church being the ten lost tribes of the house of Israel. This man talked with real authority. He talked about the transition of the church and how God had been moving the church forward since the book of Acts. But it wasn't until this major prophet of God said that we had defiled God's Sabbath and that we should repent that I began to understand and take the Sabbath more seriously.

So I got excited and came home and told my husband about the meetings. At first, my husband got excited too, because he had been the first one who tried to tell me something about the ten lost tribes of Israel. But I didn't understand the importance of it at the time. However, now I was beginning to listen.

Anyway, after I was convinced that we should be keeping the Sabbath as well as the feasts of the Lord, I tried to tell my husband. He just said over his shoulder, "Read Galatians," as if that would be enough for me to understand that this thing I was endeavoring to do was not right. Okay, so I read the book of Galatians. Of course I had read it before. But I read it again and again. You must admit that sometimes it is hard to understand the Apostle Paul.

I also told my dear old Christian friends in Montana that I was beginning to keep the Sabbath. My friend said to me over the phone, "I have a book for you to read: Galatians." So I read the book of Galatians again. I knew that I should have an answer for my well-meaning friends for why I was doing this. I also knew that if God really wants us to keep the Sabbath, then there must be something we don't understand about the Apostle Paul and his writings, and there must be some way to explain it.

So I kept searching. Finally, I found an online commentary by a Christian man who believed in keeping the Sabbath. The way he explained some of the things that Paul said helped me to finally get it. And it gave me the key to a better understanding of the writings of the Apostle Paul.

Then I noticed other Christians that were keeping the Sabbath and the Lord's feasts, and yet they also seemed to have a hard time understanding the Apostle Paul. Some people even tried to explain Paul's writings away. So I wanted to write this little book to help people understand what Paul was really talking about.

The most common opposition to keeping the law coming from Christians is when they quote the Apostle Paul. They think they have full understanding when they say, Paul said we are not under the law but under grace. Or they might say, we are not in bondage to the law. In other words, they think that keeping the Sabbath will bring us into bondage.

I like to give this analogy. A woman was driving 45 mph in a 20 mph zone. An officer of the law pulled her over. He said, "Lady, you were speeding." She said to him, "Officer, I am not under the law but under grace." And that is how most Christians view the matter today. It seems we took what Paul said about not being under the law to mean that now we are above the law.

Since, as Christians, we have been taught to believe certain things, it is often hard to change our mindset. When I showed my husband a verse (Acts 21:24) that proved that Apostle Paul continued to keep the law, even after Paul's conversion to Christ, my husband said, "Wow, it almost sounds like Paul is saying two different things."

Well, Paul was not saying two different things, we just misunderstood what he was saying. And we have been taught wrong and have developed a certain mindset. Unless we are willing to open our minds and willing to consider a different point of view, we won't get it.

In Southern California, there was a saying among Christians: "Be a Berean." There was even a Berean Christian bookstore. Who were the Bereans? The Bereans were of the town of Berea. The Bible says that the Bereans were of more noble character than the Thessalonians. When the Apostle Paul preached in the town of Thessalonica, the townsfolk went into an uproar, and Paul was forced to flee. Then Paul went and preached in the town of Berea. However, the Bereans listened to what Paul said and diligently searched the Scriptures to see if what he said was true.

Most of us understood that the Bereans were of more noble character because they studied the Scriptures. However, the other thing that set the Bereans apart was that they listened to what Paul said with readiness of mind (Acts 17:11). In other words, the Bereans had an open mind, and then they diligently searched the scriptures to see if what Paul said was true. Today, if you try telling other Christians that they should try keeping the Sabbath, oftentimes it will send those people into an uproar. If we are holding onto our old mindsets, then we don't have an open mind, and it is hard to listen. Maybe we should be more like the Bereans.

Going back to the idea of mindsets, I began to realize that most Christians are arguing from the viewpoint that the law has been done away with. They see most of the verses in the New Testament through that point of view and cannot even consider that maybe it means something else. They must just disregard what is written in what is called the Old Testament because that doesn't really satisfy their version of New Testament Christianity.

Consider what God said about the Sabbath.

> Remember the sabbath day, to keep it holy.
> Six days shalt thou labour, and do all thy work:

But the seventh day is the sabbath of the L ORD thy God: in it thou shalt not do any work, thou, nor thy son, nor thy daughter, thy manservant, nor thy maidservant, nor thy cattle, nor thy stranger that is within thy gates:

For in six days the L ORD made heaven and earth, the sea, and all that in them is, and rested the seventh day: wherefore the L ORD blessed the sabbath day, and hallowed it. (Exodus 20:8–11)

And again…

And the L ORD spake unto Moses, saying,

Speak thou also unto the children of Israel, saying, Verily my sabbaths ye shall keep: for it is a sign between me and you throughout your generations; that ye may know that I am the L ORD that doth sanctify you.

Ye shall keep the sabbath therefore; for it is holy unto you: every one that defileth it shall surely be put to death: for whosoever doeth any work therein, that soul shall be cut off from among his people.

Six days may work be done; but in the seventh is the sabbath of rest, holy to the L ORD: whosoever doeth any work in the sabbath day, he shall surely be put to death.

> Wherefore the children of Israel shall keep the sabbath, to observe the sabbath throughout their generations, for a perpetual covenant.
>
> It is a sign between me and the children of Israel for ever: for in six days the LORD made heaven and earth, and on the seventh day he rested, and was refreshed. (Exodus 31:12–17)

Did you notice the words "remember the Sabbath" and "throughout your generations" and "for a perpetual covenant"? And did you see the words *for ever* in the above verse? Did you notice that God was very serious about the Sabbath and said that anyone who did any work on that day should be put to death? Well, we all probably have worked on the Sabbath, so we all deserve death, right? That is what the Bible says, but I am getting ahead of myself.

What about these other verses also found in what is called the Old Testament? Please notice the words *everlasting covenant* in the following examples:

> And the bow shall be in the cloud; and I will look upon it, that I may remember the everlasting covenant between God and every living creature of all flesh that is upon the earth. (Genesis 9:16)

God made an everlasting covenant with all flesh starting in Noah's time. He put the rainbow in the cloud as a sign or a token of his covenant. Today the rainbow can still be seen in the clouds on a rainy day. God also made an everlasting covenant with Abraham and his seed. Circumcision is a sign or token of the covenant God made with Abraham. And circumcision is still practiced today.

> And I will establish my covenant between me and thee and thy seed after thee in their generations for an everlasting covenant, to be a God unto thee, and to thy seed after thee. (Genesis 17:7)

> He that is born in thy house, and he that is bought with thy money, must needs be circumcised: and my covenant shall be in your flesh for an everlasting covenant. (Genesis 17:13)

> And God said, Sarah thy wife shall bear thee a son indeed; and thou shalt call his name Isaac: and I will establish my covenant with him for an everlasting covenant, and with his seed after him. (Genesis 17:19)

God promised Abraham an heir and his son Isaac was born to Sarah. God also established his covenant with Isaac and his seed after him. And that covenant was an everlasting covenant.

Furthermore, many years later, God made a covenant with King David as well.

> I have made a covenant with my chosen, I have sworn unto David my servant,

> Thy seed will I establish for ever,
> and build up thy throne to all genera-
> tions. Selah. (Psalm 89:3–4)

See also the following:

> Incline your ear, and come unto me:
> hear, and your soul shall live; and I will
> make an everlasting covenant with you,
> even the sure mercies of David. (Isaiah
> 55:3 KJV)

Do you think that Jesus came to abolish the everlasting covenant that God made with our forefathers Abraham, Isaac, and Jacob?

Jesus said,

> Think not that I am come to destroy
> the law, or the prophets: I am not come
> to destroy, but to fulfil. For verily I say
> unto you, Till heaven and earth pass, one
> jot or one tittle shall in no wise pass from
> the law, till all be fulfilled. (Matthew
> 5:17–18)

Jesus said he didn't come to destroy the law or the prophets. If you think that the law has passed away, then you might want to consider that you have a certain mindset. It is possible we have been taught some things that are not quite right.

Of course, a lot of Christians want to point out that Jesus said he came to fulfill the law. Yes, but are you listening? How many times did Jesus say, let him who has ears to hear,

hear? If you can't hear it, maybe you should consider that you have a certain mindset.

Jesus fulfilled the law by becoming the sacrifice for our sins. Now we can go to heaven. He also said, until heaven and earth pass, not one jot or tittle shall pass from the law till all be fulfilled. Has heaven or earth passed?

Another thing Jesus said is that you can't pour new wine into old wineskins, or it will burst the skins. If your mind is already made up, and you think you already know everything about God and the Bible, then you are not open to learning anything new. You must be able to expand your mind for you to hear. If you want to change your mindset, then you should probably fast and pray and ask God to give you ears to hear.

This *is* a faithful saying and worthy of all
acceptance, that Christ Jesus came into the
world to save sinners, of whom I am chief.

—Apostle Paul, 1 Timothy 1:15 NKJV

The law of the LORD is perfect, converting the
soul: the testimony of the LORD is sure,
making wise the simple.

—Psalm 19:7

Chapter 1

Whenever one talks about keeping the Sabbath or the feasts of the Lord, often other Christians will say, read Galatians. Or they might say, "Paul said we are not under the law but under grace." Or some might tell us that we have liberty now and are not in bondage to the law. Let us look at the book of Galatians and see if we can understand what the Apostle Paul was really talking about.

Turn to the first chapter of Galatians and read verses 1–8. Paul was an apostle called by Jesus Christ and God the Father. Paul was not called by man. He wrote this letter to the churches in Galatia.

> Paul, an apostle, (not of men, neither by man, but by Jesus Christ, and God the Father, who raised him from the dead;)
>
> And all the brethren which are with me, unto the churches of Galatia:
>
> Grace be to you and peace from God the Father, and from our Lord Jesus Christ. (Galatians 1:1–3)

I marvel that ye are so soon removed from him that called you into the grace of Christ unto another gospel:

Which is not another; but there be some that trouble you, and would pervert the gospel of Christ.

But though we, or an angel from heaven, preach any other gospel unto you than that which we have preached unto you, let him be accursed. (Galatians 1:6–8)

The apostle was amazed that the Galatians were so quickly led astray from him that called them into the grace of Christ unto another gospel. Apparently, some people were trying to pervert the gospel. The apostle wanted to make it clear that preaching a different gospel than the one ordained of God is a serious offense. In fact, Paul said that whoever teaches a different gospel should be accursed.

Now go to down to verse 11.

But I certify you, brethren, that the gospel which was preached of me is not after man.

For I neither received it of man, neither was I taught it, but by the revelation of Jesus Christ.

For ye have heard of my conversation in time past in the Jews' religion, how that beyond measure I persecuted the church of God, and wasted it:

And profited in the Jews' religion above many my equals in mine own nation, being more exceedingly zealous of the traditions of my fathers.

But when it pleased God, who separated me from my mother's womb, and called me by his grace,

To reveal his Son in me, that I might preach him among the heathen; immediately I conferred not with flesh and blood:

Neither went I up to Jerusalem to them which were apostles before me; but I went into Arabia, and returned again unto Damascus.

Then after three years I went up to Jerusalem to see Peter, and abode with him fifteen days. (verses 11–18)

We can see here that the gospel Paul preached was not from man. Paul did not learn it from men. The gospel was revealed to him by God. Paul said he did not confer with flesh and blood (verse 16). In other words, he didn't go and ask other people what they thought. Paul didn't even go to the first apostles to talk to them. Paul said he went to Arabia, and apparently, he sought the Lord there by himself. Then three years later, Paul went to see the Apostle Peter.

Paul said he received the gospel by revelation. Remember the time Simon Peter made his confession of faith? Jesus asked his disciples who they thought he was. Peter declared that he was the Christ, the Son of the living God. Jesus told Peter that he was blessed because flesh and blood had not revealed it to him but his Father in heaven. (Matthew 16:17). And that was how the Apostle Paul received the gospel. It was revealed to him by God.

Let's go back to the story as Paul was telling it to the Galatians. Go to chapter 2 of Galatians. The Apostle Paul went up to Jerusalem fourteen years later. He said he went by revelation.

> Then fourteen years after I went up again to Jerusalem with Barnabas, and took Titus with me also.
>
> And I went up by revelation, and communicated unto them that gospel which I preach among the Gentiles, but privately to them which were of reputation, lest by any means I should run, or had run, in vain.
>
> But neither Titus, who was with me, being a Greek, was compelled to be circumcised:
>
> And that because of false brethren unawares brought in, who came in privily to spy out our liberty which we have in Christ Jesus,
>
> To whom we gave place by subjection, no, not for an hour; that the truth of the gospel might continue with you. (Galatians 2:1–5)

Paul said that they did not give in, not even for a moment, that the truth of the gospel might continue with you. What is the truth of the gospel? Apart from the gospels themselves, most of the teachings about the gospel found in the New Testament come from the writings of the Apostle Paul. In fact, Paul even called it *his* gospel (Romans 2:16, 2 Timothy 2:8). And that is interesting since Paul's conversion to Christ happened after Jesus died and rose again. Paul did not walk with Jesus while Christ was on the earth, like those first disciples did.

So what do we know about the Apostle Paul? He was known as Saul of Tarsus. From his writings, we learned that he was an Israelite of the tribe of Benjamin and circumcised on the eighth day. And Paul was very careful to keep the law, and he was a Pharisee. In fact, Paul was tutored by Gamaliel, a respected Pharisee and leading rabbi in the Sanhedrin. In his letter to the Galatians, Paul said that he profited in the Jews' religion above many others because he was very zealous for the tradition of his fathers. Furthermore, Paul told us, he persecuted the church of God and wasted it.

Paul was there when Stephen was stoned to death and even consented to his death. In Acts 8:3, we read that Paul wreaked havoc upon the church and entered homes and caused men and women to be hauled off to prison. Paul had obtained letters from the high priest to the synagogues, giving him authority to take to prison any who were found to be following the way (of Jesus). But while he was on the way to Damascus, suddenly they were surrounded by a bright light, and Paul fell to the earth, and he heard the Lord speaking to him and saying, "Saul, Saul, why are you persecuting me?" On the road to Damascus, Saul encountered the living Christ. And so Saul was converted, and now we know him as the Apostle Paul.

After his conversion, Paul sought the Lord. And he received understanding of the gospel by revelation from the Lord. Later, Paul went to see Peter and then the other apostles. And even though Paul had previously persecuted the church, Paul was accepted by those first apostles. In fact, Paul communicated with Peter and the others the gospel that he taught and obtained their blessing to go and preach.

Let's continue further. As we have been reading Paul's letter to the Galatians, we see that he is recounting the events as they happened. First, he was called by God's grace to preach about his Son, Jesus Christ. Then he sought the Lord and received the gospel by revelation from God. Then Paul went to see the Apostle Peter and stayed with him fifteen days. After that, Paul talked about going up to Jerusalem.

In Jerusalem, Paul met with the other disciples and communicated with them the gospel that he preached. The events that happened in Jerusalem described here in the book of Galatians appear to be the same events in Jerusalem that are described in Acts, chapter 15, which some Bibles refer to as the council at Jerusalem.

To get a better understanding of what happened in Jerusalem, we need to read the account from the book of Acts. Turn to Acts 15:1–21. Let's see what took place at the council at Jerusalem.

> And certain men which came down from Judaea taught the brethren, and said, Except ye be circumcised after the manner of Moses, ye cannot be saved.
>
> When therefore Paul and Barnabas had no small dissension and disputation with them, they determined that Paul and Barnabas, and certain other of them, should go up to Jerusalem unto the apostles and elders about this question. (Acts 15:1–2)

Certain men were teaching that unless the new Gentile converts were circumcised, they could not be saved. Paul and Barnabas obviously did not agree with what those men were teaching, or they wouldn't have been disputing with them. And it was not just a small disagreement. The matter was of such importance that it was decided that Paul and Barnabas and others should go up to Jerusalem so that the matter in question could be settled by the apostles and elders.

> And when they were come to Jerusalem, they were received of the church, and of the apostles and elders, and they declared all things that God had done with them. But there rose up certain of the sect of the Pharisees which believed, saying, That it was needful to circumcise them, and to command them to keep the law of Moses.
> And the apostles and elders came together for to consider of this matter. (Acts 15:4–6)

What was the matter to consider? The matter in question was what some of the Pharisees were teaching the new Gentile converts.

> Except ye be circumcised after the manner of Moses, ye cannot be saved. (Acts 15:1)

The matter in question was not whether these new Gentile converts should be circumcised and keep the law of Moses. The matter in question was whether they had to be circumcised first as a requirement before they could be saved. Some Pharisees were saying that unless the new Gentile converts were circumcised, they could not be saved.

> And the apostles and elders came together for to consider of this matter. And when there had been much disput-

ing, Peter rose up, and said unto them, Men and brethren, ye know how that a good while ago God made choice among us, that the Gentiles by my mouth should hear the word of the gospel, and believe. And God, which knoweth the hearts, bare them witness, giving them the Holy Ghost, even as he did unto us; And put no difference between us and them, purifying their hearts by faith. Now therefore why tempt ye God, to put a yoke upon the neck of the disciples, which neither our fathers nor we were able to bear? But we believe that through the grace of the Lord Jesus Christ we shall be saved, even as they. (Acts 15:6–11)

See Acts, chapter 10, for the story when the Apostle Peter received a vision of unclean animals, and he was told to get up and kill and eat them. Peter told the Lord he never ate anything unclean. The Lord told Peter not to call unclean what God had cleansed. After he had the vision, Peter was led to go and preach to the Gentiles. Peter told the Gentiles the good news about Jesus and said that whoever believed in him would receive remission of sins. When Peter finished preaching, the gift of the Holy Ghost was poured out upon the Gentiles.

When Peter saw that Holy Ghost was poured out upon the Gentiles, Peter understood from his vision that God had purified the hearts of those Gentiles, and he was not to call them unclean. In those days, the Gentiles were considered unclean and were not instructed in the law of Moses. And yet, the Holy Ghost was given to them, even as it was given to the Jews in the upper room.

Speaking to the others at the council in Jerusalem, Peter said they should not tempt God by putting a yoke on the new converts, for they knew that neither they (the Jews) nor their forefathers were able to keep all the law without sin. Peter declared that it is through the grace of the Lord Jesus that we are saved (Acts 15:11).

Let's go and look at Paul's letter to Romans 3:1–31. Start in verses 1 and 2.

> What advantage then hath the Jew?
> or what profit is there of circumcision?
> Much every way: chiefly, because
> that unto them were committed the ora-
> cles of God.

Paul said the Jews had an advantage because they were given the responsibility of keeping the oracles of God. The Bible has often been referred to as God's word. The Jews kept the Scriptures.

Now go down to verse 9 and continue reading from there.

> What then? are we better than they?
> No, in no wise: for we have before proved
> both Jews and Gentiles, that they are all
> under sin;
> As it is written, There is none righ-
> teous, no, not one:
> There is none that understandeth,
> there is none that seeketh after God.
> They are all gone out of the way,
> they are together become unprofitable;
> there is none that doeth good, no, not
> one.

> Their throat is an open sepulchre;
> with their tongues they have used deceit;
> the poison of asps is under their lips:
> Whose mouth is full of cursing and
> bitterness:
> Their feet are swift to shed blood:
> Destruction and misery are in their
> ways:
> And the way of peace have they not
> known:
> There is no fear of God before their
> eyes. (verses 9–18)

Above, in verse 10, we read, "As it is written…" Paul was quoting from the Scriptures. Those early apostles were all Jews, and as Jews, they were instructed in the law. And the Scriptures said that there are none that are righteous. Continue reading.

> Now we know that what things soever the law saith, it saith to them who are under the law: that every mouth may be stopped, and all the world may become guilty before God.
> Therefore by the deeds of the law there shall no flesh be justified in his sight: for by the law is the knowledge of sin.
> But now the righteousness of God without the law is manifested, being witnessed by the law and the prophets;
> Even the righteousness of God which is by faith of Jesus Christ unto all and upon all them that believe: for there is no difference:

> For all have sinned, and come short of the glory of God;
>
> Being justified freely by his grace through the redemption that is in Christ Jesus:
>
> Whom God hath set forth to be a propitiation through faith in his blood, to declare his righteousness for the remission of sins that are past, through the forbearance of God. (verses 19–25)

In other words, Paul said that the law speaks to those under its authority, so that every mouth may be stopped, and all the world may become guilty before God. Therefore, by our own deeds, no one will be justified in his sight. For we all have sinned and fallen short of God's glory.

But now, Paul said, a righteousness of God without the law has been manifested, which was witnessed by the law and the prophets. In other words, it was told about in the Scriptures. Paul spoke about the righteousness of God that comes by faith in Jesus Christ to all those that believe, for all have sinned and fallen short of the glory of God. But we are justified freely by grace through faith in Jesus and his blood that was shed. Praise God. We are saved by God's grace.

Okay, let's go back to the story. We started in Galatians, then we looked in the book of Acts, and we read about the events that took place at the council in Jerusalem. And we have gained more insight into what happened in Jerusalem. Now let's go back again to the second chapter of Galatians and read from that account once more.

> Then fourteen years after I went up again to Jerusalem with Barnabas, and took Titus with me also.

And I went up by revelation, and communicated unto them that gospel which I preach among the Gentiles, but privately to them which were of reputation, lest by any means I should run, or had run, in vain.

But neither Titus, who was with me, being a Greek, was compelled to be circumcised:

And that because of false brethren unawares brought in, who came in privily to spy out our liberty which we have in Christ Jesus,

To whom we gave place by subjection, no, not for an hour; that the truth of the gospel might continue with you. (Galatians 2:1–5)

Certain men said that the new Gentile converts needed to be circumcised before they could be saved. Paul and his companions did not give in to the pressure from these false brethren. They did not have Titus get circumcised. Paul needed to preserve the truth of the gospel.

The Apostle Paul was not teaching against circumcision or the law. They were trying to prove a point. They had to establish the fact that we are saved by grace. Paul and Barnabas did not give in and have Titus circumcised so that the truth of the gospel might be established. What is the truth of the gospel? The truth of the gospel is that we are saved by grace through faith. We have all sinned and fallen short of God's glory. But God, in his love, gave us his Son, Yeshua (Jesus), who died for our sins so that we can be saved.

For by grace are ye saved through faith; and that not of yourselves: it is the

gift of God: Not of works, lest any man
should boast. (Ephesians 2:8–9)

The Pharisees wanted to add circumcision as a requirement to being saved. We are saved by grace, not by our own
works in keeping the law. It is not because of our ability to
keep the law or anything we have done. When Jesus was
dying on the cross, the thief on a cross next to him asked
Jesus to remember him when he came into his kingdom.
Jesus told the thief that he would be with him that very day
in paradise. (It's a good thing Jesus didn't tell the thief he had
to go get circumcised first.)

Now look in the book of Romans, chapter 3, again and
continue to the end of the chapter. Notice verse 28. It says a
man is justified by faith without the deeds of the law.

> Being justified freely by his grace
> through the redemption that is in Christ
> Jesus:
> Whom God hath set forth to be a
> propitiation through faith in his blood,
> to declare his righteousness for the remis-
> sion of sins that are past, through the for-
> bearance of God;
> To declare, I say, at this time his
> righteousness: that he might be just, and
> the justifier of him which believeth in
> Jesus.
> Where is boasting then? It is
> excluded. By what law? of works? Nay:
> but by the law of faith.
> Therefore we conclude that a man
> is justified by faith without the deeds of
> the law.

Is he the God of the Jews only? is he not also of the Gentiles? Yes, of the Gentiles also:

Seeing it is one God, which shall justify the circumcision by faith, and uncircumcision through faith.

Do we then make void the law through faith? God forbid: yea, we establish the law. (Romans 3:24–31)

It does not matter whether you are a Jew or a Gentile. We have all sinned and fallen short of God's holiness. The good news is that we can be saved by faith in Jesus Christ and his death on the cross. He paid the penalty for our sins, and we can't add anything to that. Salvations is a gift from God.

Does that mean we should not try to keep the law? The Apostle Paul asked, "Do we make void the law through faith?" In other words, now that we have faith in Jesus, do we get rid of the law? God forbid, Paul said. On the contrary, we establish the law.

The statutes of the LORD are right, rejoicing
the heart: the commandment of the
LORD is pure, enlightening the eyes.

—Psalm 19:8

Chapter 2

As a review of chapter one, we started in the book of Galatians and learned several things. We learned that Paul was an apostle of God. Paul said, the gospel that he preached, he received by revelation from God. And then the apostle took a stand to preserve the truth of the gospel. Afterward, we turned to Acts, chapter 15, and read about the events that occurred at the council of Jerusalem.

Now when we look at what happened at the council of Jerusalem and realize what the early apostles taught, then we can understand the Apostle Paul and his writings better. Let's review what took place at the council of Jerusalem. The gospel had been preached to the Gentiles. Certain Pharisees began to teach that the Gentile converts needed to be circumcised first before they could be saved. Paul and Barnabas disagreed with what those men were teaching, so they disputed with those Pharisees. Finally, they went up to Jerusalem, where the matter was settled by the apostles and elders. Peter declared that we are saved by the grace of the Lord Jesus. (See Acts 15:11.)

Let's read further about what happened at the council in Jerusalem in Acts 15:12–21.

> Then all the multitude kept silence, and gave audience to Barnabas and Paul, declaring what miracles and wonders God had wrought among the Gentiles by them.
>
> And after they had held their peace, James answered, saying, Men and brethren, hearken unto me:
>
> Simeon hath declared how God at the first did visit the Gentiles, to take out of them a people for his name.
>
> And to this agree the words of the prophets; as it is written,
>
> After this I will return, and will build again the tabernacle of David, which is fallen down; and I will build again the ruins thereof, and I will set it up:
>
> That the residue of men might seek after the Lord, and all the Gentiles, upon whom my name is called, saith the Lord, who doeth all these things.
>
> Known unto God are all his works from the beginning of the world.
>
> Wherefore my sentence is, that we trouble not them, which from among the Gentiles are turned to God:
>
> But that we write unto them, that they abstain from pollutions of idols, and from fornication, and from things strangled, and from blood.

> For Moses of old time hath in every
> city them that preach him, being read in
> the synagogues every sabbath day.

James was careful to point out that the scriptures foretold that the Gentiles would turn to the Lord. Jesus had already come and died and rose from the dead and gone on to heaven. The disciples were going on into new territory. And since it was obvious from the miracles that were being done that God was visiting the Gentiles, it was also a good thing to know that it had been prophesied beforehand in the Scriptures. We can see that the early apostles wanted to "do it by the book," as the saying goes.

James agreed with Peter that they should not lay a heavy burden on the new converts. James said that the Gentiles should begin by doing those first four things—abstain from pollution of idols, fornication, things strangled, and from blood—because James said, Moses is taught in the synagogues on the Sabbath (see verse 21). In other words, the Gentile converts could learn more about the law as they came into the synagogues.

Suppose, in modern times, God begins to move in a mighty way among the street people. Suddenly, all kinds of people—including drug addicts, pimps, and prostitutes, thieves, and the like—start pouring into the churches. The church leaders would probably want to lay down some basic rules for those people as they came in to learn more about God. They might give them some rules, like, "Okay, stop stealing. Don't sleep around, and we will help you get cleaned up and delivered from drugs."

Those early apostles saw that God was opening the way for the Gentiles to come in and learn about the God of Abraham, Isaac, and Jacob. The Gentiles did not know how to serve this holy God. So the disciples decided it was necessary to require that the Gentile converts begin by learning some basic rules. The apostles never said that the new believers did not need to keep the law.

Now let's go back to Acts 15 and the council of Jerusalem. The apostles wrote letters to the early churches with instructions for the new gentile believers.

> And they wrote letters by them after this manner; The apostles and elders and brethren send greeting unto the brethren which are of the Gentiles in Antioch and Syria and Cilicia.
>
> Forasmuch as we have heard, that certain which went out from us have troubled you with words, subverting your souls, saying, Ye must be circumcised, and keep the law: to whom we gave no such commandment:
>
> It seemed good unto us, being assembled with one accord, to send chosen men unto you with our beloved Barnabas and Paul,
>
> Men that have hazarded their lives for the name of our Lord Jesus Christ.
>
> We have sent therefore Judas and Silas, who shall also tell you the same things by mouth.
>
> For it seemed good to the Holy Ghost, and to us, to lay upon you no greater burden than these necessary things;
>
> That ye abstain from meats offered to idols, and from blood, and from things strangled, and from fornication: from

which if ye keep yourselves, ye shall do
well. Fare ye well. (Acts 15:23–29)

The apostles wrote the letters with the instructions for the new converts and sent them with Barnabas and Paul. While they were on their way, Paul met Timothy and wanted him to go with them. Paul had Timothy circumcised, and then afterward, they delivered the letters from the apostles and elders. (See Acts 16:1–4.)

> Him would Paul have to go forth with him; and took and circumcised him because of the Jews which were in those quarters: for they knew all that his father was a Greek.
>
> And as they went through the cities, they delivered them the decrees for to keep, that were ordained of the apostles and elders which were at Jerusalem. (Acts 16:3–4)

While they were on their way, carrying the letters with the decrees from the elders, they met Timothy. Paul wanted him to go with them, so he had Timothy circumcised. Do you think, if the letters were teaching against circumcision or the law, Paul would have had Timothy get circumcised? The letters simply contained instructions for the new believers. The letters did not say they were not to be circumcised. The letters contained the first four rules for the new converts to follow. The apostles expected that the Gentiles could learn about Moses and the law as they came into the synagogues. (See above, Acts 15:19–21.)

Okay, now that we have read in the book of Acts about what happened at the council in Jerusalem, let's go back again to Paul's account in his letter to the Galatians and continue reading from there.

> And when James, Cephas, and John, who seemed to be pillars, perceived the grace that was given unto me, they gave to me and Barnabas the right hands of fellowship; that we should go unto the heathen, and they unto the circumcision.
>
> Only they would that we should remember the poor; the same which I also was forward to do.
>
> But when Peter was come to Antioch, I withstood him to the face, because he was to be blamed.
>
> For before that certain came from James, he did eat with the Gentiles: but when they were come, he withdrew and separated himself, fearing them which were of the circumcision.
>
> And the other Jews dissembled likewise with him; insomuch that Barnabas also was carried away with their dissimulation.
>
> But when I saw that they walked not uprightly according to the truth of the gospel, I said unto Peter before them all, If thou, being a Jew, livest after the manner of Gentiles, and not as do the Jews, why compellest thou the Gentiles to live as do the Jews? (Galatians 2:9–14)

Paul said they were not walking uprightly according to the truth of the gospel (verse 14). Once again, the Apostle

Paul made a stand for the truth of the gospel. Remember that it was Peter who had been given a vision and told that he was not to call unclean what God had cleansed. And yet, even though Peter had begun to eat meals with the new Gentile believers, when James and certain other Jews showed up, Peter separated himself from the Gentiles, as if they were not acceptable. (Jews did not usually eat with Gentiles because they were considered unclean.) Paul rebuked Peter before them all, and then he reminded them that we are justified by faith in Jesus and not by the works of the law.

Continue reading.

> We who are Jews by nature, and not sinners of the Gentiles,
>
> Knowing that a man is not justified by the works of the law, but by the faith of Jesus
>
> Christ, even we have believed in Jesus Christ, that we might be justified by the faith of Christ, and not by the works of the law: for by the works of the law shall no flesh be justified.
>
> But if, while we seek to be justified by Christ, we ourselves also are found sinners, is therefore Christ the minister of sin? God forbid.
>
> For if I build again the things which I destroyed, I make myself a transgressor.
>
> For I through the law am dead to the law, that I might live unto God.
>
> I am crucified with Christ: nevertheless I live; yet not I, but Christ liveth in me: and the life which I now live in the

flesh I live by the faith of the Son of God,
who loved me, and gave himself for me.

I do not frustrate the grace of God:
for if righteousness come by the law,
then Christ is dead in vain. (Galatians
2:15–21)

Even the Jews that had come to believe in Jesus knew that they had fallen short of keeping the law and sought to be justified by faith. For it says, by the works of the law shall no flesh be justified. If the Israelites could have obtained righteousness by their own merits, then there would have been no need for sacrifices for sins and therefore, also, no reason for Christ to die.

Paul said he did not frustrate the grace of God. If we could have obtained righteousness by keeping the law, then Jesus died in vain. However, we have all sinned and fallen short of God's glory or holiness. Therefore, we could never be good enough to be saved by our own efforts. That is why we must simply accept the gift of salvation that has been offered by God through Jesus Christ. If we were to rely on ourselves and our own ability to keep the law, then no one could be saved. But thank God, Jesus came and died for our sins to make a way for us to be saved.

Now let's go back and look again at Galatians 2:19–20.

For I through the law am dead to
the law, that I might live unto God.

I am crucified with Christ: nevertheless I live; yet not I, but Christ liveth
in me: and the life which I now live in the
flesh I live by the faith of the Son of God,
who loved me, and gave himself for me.

Paul said he was dead to the law, that he might live unto God.

Let's go to the book of Romans, chapter 7, and look at verses 4 through 12.

> Wherefore, my brethren, ye also are become dead to the law by the body of Christ; that ye should be married to another, even to him who is raised from the dead, that we should bring forth fruit unto God.
>
> For when we were in the flesh, the motions of sins, which were by the law, did work in our members to bring forth fruit unto death.
>
> But now we are delivered from the law, that being dead wherein we were held; that we should serve in newness of spirit, and not in the oldness of the letter.
>
> What shall we say then? Is the law sin? God forbid. Nay, I had not known sin, but by the law: for I had not known lust, except the law had said, Thou shalt not covet.
>
> But sin, taking occasion by the commandment, wrought in me all manner of concupiscence. For without the law sin was dead.
>
> For I was alive without the law once: but when the commandment came, sin revived, and I died.
>
> And the commandment, which was ordained to life, I found to be unto death.

> For sin, taking occasion by the com-
> mandment, deceived me, and by it slew
> me.
> Wherefore the law is holy, and the
> commandment holy, and just, and good.

Paul said that sin slew him because of the commandment. Sin brings death because of the law. Adam and Eve sinned when they ate fruit from the tree in the garden. God told them not to eat from that tree, and when they disobeyed God, it brought forth death. Since God gave the law, and we broke the law, we have all sinned, and we all deserve death. When we accept Jesus as our Savior, we are also accepting Christ's death on the cross in our behalf. That is what Paul meant when he said that he was crucified with Christ.

Now look at verse 7. Paul asked if the law was sin—no, for we would not have known we were sinners if it were not for the law. For example, the law said that we should not lie. Therefore, if we have ever lied, then we have sinned and broken the law. The law defines what a sin is, so the law is not sin. In fact, Paul said the law is holy, and the commandment is holy and just and good.

Now let's go back and look again at the verse in Romans 7:6.

> But now we are delivered from the
> law, that being dead wherein we were
> held; that we should serve in newness of
> spirit, and not in the oldness of the letter.

Hopefully, now we can understand what Paul meant to be delivered from the law and to be dead to the law. He goes on to say we should serve in the newness of the spirit, not in the oldness of the letter. He was talking about the letter of the law. The letter kills, but the spirit gives life (2 Corinthians 3:5–6). That does not mean we do not keep the commandments. However, now we can live and keep the commandments in the spirit of the law without becoming legalistic about it.

The Pharisees were being legalistic when they kept trying to accuse Jesus of breaking the law. They accused him when he healed on the Sabbath. Jesus taught them that it is all right to do good on the Sabbath. Jesus also said it's okay to pull your ox out of the ditch on the Sabbath if necessary. And when his disciples were hungry and picked corn to eat on the Sabbath, Jesus stood up for his disciples and said that the Sabbath was made for man, not man for the Sabbath. Jesus is Lord of the Sabbath.

The church, for the most part, got it right that we are sinners and that we are saved by grace through faith in Jesus Christ. However, many Christians misunderstood the Apostle Paul and the early apostles. We misunderstood and thought that it wasn't necessary to keep the law anymore. The church keeps parts of the law, but most Christians forget about the Sabbath, as well as the new moons and the feasts of the Lord.

Nowadays, if you ask a Christian if we are supposed to keep the Ten Commandments, they will probably say yes. Then if you ask them about the Sabbath, they might say, "Well, we keep Sunday Sabbath, or any day is fine, or we worship God every day." God said to remember the Sabbath, yet it has been mostly forgotten by the church.

We Christians have been missing so much. We have been worshipping God according to our traditions. We faithfully kept Christmas and Easter and other holidays that have pagan roots, and yet we forgot the holy days that God commanded should be kept. Jesus rebuked the Pharisees in his day because they put their traditions above the commandments of God. See the story in Mark, chapter 7, and Matthew 15.

> Hypocrites! Well did Isaiah prophesy about you, saying:
> "These people [c]draw near to Me with their mouth,
> And honor Me with *their* lips,
> But their heart is far from Me.
> And in vain they worship Me,
> Teaching *as* doctrines the commandments of men." (Matthew 15:7–9 NKJV)

The Lord was quoting from the prophet Isaiah.

> For the LORD hath poured out upon you the spirit of deep sleep, and hath closed your eyes: the prophets and your rulers, the seers hath he covered.
> And the vision of all is become unto you as the words of a book that is sealed, which men deliver to one that is learned, saying, Read this, I pray thee: and he saith, I cannot; for it is sealed:
> And the book is delivered to him that is not learned, saying, Read this, I pray thee: and he saith, I am not learned.
> Wherefore the Lord said, Forasmuch as this people draw near me with their mouth, and with their lips do honour me, but have removed their heart far from me, and their fear toward me is taught by the precept of men: (Isaiah 29:10–13 KJV)

The fear of the LORD is clean, enduring
for ever: the judgments of the LORD
are true and righteous altogether.

—Psalm 19:9

Chapter 3

When you look at the book of Galatians in the light of the fact that the early apostles did not teach against keeping the law, things get a bit easier to understand. Once again, the apostles and elders settled the matter that we are saved by grace through faith in Jesus Christ; not by our own works in keeping the law. See Acts, chapter 15, about the council of Jerusalem.

Now let's move on in Galatians. In Galatians, chapter 3, the Apostle Paul calls the Galatians foolish and even bewitched.

> O foolish Galatians, who hath bewitched you, that ye should not obey the truth, before whose eyes Jesus Christ hath been evidently set forth, crucified among you?
>
> This only would I learn of you, Received ye the Spirit by the works of the law, or by the hearing of faith?
>
> Are ye so foolish? having begun in the Spirit, are ye now made perfect by the flesh? (Galatians 3:1–3)

27

There is a saying that goes, "Not all that glitters is gold." Have you ever heard of fool's gold? Fool's gold can often be seen on the surface in the sand, along the shores of rivers and streams. Fool's gold is just iron pyrite. Real gold is nineteen times heavier than water. Real gold weighs more than fool's gold and sinks below the surface and continues to work its way down through the sand and gravel, even down to the bedrock. So if you want to find the real gold, you must dig deeper.

We Christians have been looking at Galatians with a wrong mindset. The Apostle Paul was very learned in the law. We took things that Paul said and looked at them just on the surface and thought we understood everything. Paul's writings are very deep. So if we want to understand what he taught, then we must be willing to open our minds and learn.

These verses in Galatians are where a lot of Christians have stumbled. We looked at those verses and assumed that Paul was saying, "Who has bewitched you? We don't keep the law anymore?" There is nothing further from the truth! We have been missing the point.

Paul said, those Galatians were foolish and bewitched. They had obviously been taught about Christ's death on the cross and believed. However, after beginning in the Spirit, they were trying to go back to being made perfect by the flesh. Paul was talking about faith. He was talking about having faith toward God. In other words, he was saying, "Did you get here because you kept the law or because you came by faith?"

When we first realized that we were sinners before God and accepted Jesus as our Savior, we began a new life in Christ. Jesus said, "I am the way, the truth, and the life. No one comes to the Father but by me." Now we can have access to God the Father. Now we can have a relationship with this holy, living God! Now we can have our sins washed away, and we can have eternal life. Now that we have accepted Jesus and have asked forgiveness for our sins, are we going to go back and start trusting in our own self-righteousness?

Consider the parable about the Pharisee and the publican. Jesus told a parable that showed the difference between the one who trusts in his own righteousness or religion and one who realizes his own sins and need of mercy. The Pharisee boasted and trusted in his own works and thought he was acceptable to God. Meanwhile, the publican stood afar off and asked God to be merciful to him because he was a sinner. Jesus said that it was the publican who went home justified before God.

> Also He spoke this parable to some who trusted in themselves that they were righteous, and despised others: "Two men went up to the temple to pray, one a Pharisee and the other a tax collector. The Pharisee stood and prayed thus with himself, 'God, I thank You that I am not like other men—extortioners, unjust, adulterers, or even as this tax collector. I fast twice a week; I give tithes of all that I possess.' And the tax collector, standing afar off, would not so much as raise *his* eyes to heaven, but beat his breast, saying, 'God, be merciful to me a sinner!' I tell you, this man went down to his house justified *rather* than the other; for everyone who exalts himself will be [d] humbled, and he who humbles himself will be exalted." (Luke 18:9–14 NKJV)

Let's go back to Galatians and read what it is said once more.

> O foolish Galatians, who hath bewitched you, that ye should not obey the truth, before whose eyes Jesus Christ hath been evidently set forth, crucified among you?
>
> This only would I learn of you, Received ye the Spirit by the works of the law, or by the hearing of faith?
>
> Are ye so foolish? having begun in the Spirit, are ye now made perfect by the flesh? (Galatians 3:1–3)

Continue on.

> Have ye suffered so many things in vain? if it be yet in vain.
>
> He therefore that ministereth to you the Spirit, and worketh miracles among you, doeth he it by the works of the law, or by the hearing of faith?
>
> Even as Abraham believed God, and it was accounted to him for righteousness.
>
> Know ye therefore that they which are of faith, the same are the children of Abraham. (Galatians 3:4–7)

Now let's go look at Roman 4:1–14.

> What shall we say then that Abraham our father, as pertaining to the flesh, hath found?

For if Abraham were justified by works, he hath whereof to glory; but not before God. For what saith the scripture? Abraham believed God, and it was counted unto him for righteousness. Now to him that worketh is the reward not reckoned of grace, but of debt. But to him that worketh not, but believeth on him that justifieth the ungodly, his faith is counted for righteousness. (Romans 4:1–5)

If you work for something, your reward comes because you earned it. It's just like when you worked for a paycheck. But if you only believed God and then your faith was counted for righteousness, then that is grace. You didn't earn it.

Even as David also describeth the blessedness of the man, unto whom God imputeth righteousness without works,

Saying, Blessed are they whose iniquities are forgiven, and whose sins are covered.

Blessed is the man to whom the Lord will not impute sin.

Cometh this blessedness then upon the circumcision only, or upon the uncircumcision also? for we say that faith was reckoned to Abraham for righteousness.

How was it then reckoned? when he was in circumcision, or in uncircumcision? Not in circumcision, but in uncircumcision.

And he received the sign of circumcision, a seal of the righteousness of the faith which he had yet being uncircumcised: that he might be the father of all them that believe, though they be not circumcised; that righteousness might be imputed unto them also:

And the father of circumcision to them who are not of the circumcision only, but who also walk in the steps of that faith of our father Abraham, which he had being yet uncircumcised.

For the promise, that he should be the heir of the world, was not to Abraham, or to his seed, through the law, but through the righteousness of faith.

For if they which are of the law be heirs, faith is made void, and the promise made of none effect: (Romans 4:6–14)

King David said that those whose sins are forgiven are blessed. Is this blessedness only for the circumcised—in other words, the Jews? No, it is for the Gentiles as well.

Paul said Abraham is the father of circumcision. Did Abraham receive the promise before or after he was circumcised? Abraham received the promise *first*, and then he got circumcised. Circumcision then became a sign or a token of the covenant.

Abraham believed God, and it was counted unto him for righteousness. Abraham received the sign of circumcision so that he might be the father of all of them that believe, whether circumcised or not. We then that have believed and have put our trust in Jesus are blessed with Father Abraham.

In verses 13 and 14 above, the apostle said that the promise to Abraham and to his seed to be the heir of the world was not through the law but through faith. Now we can see that Abraham is our example. He believed God, and it was counted to him as righteousness. Likewise, we believed God when we were convicted of sin and accepted Jesus as our Savior. Then our faith in Jesus was counted for righteousness.

Now go back to Galatians, chapter 3, and continue with verses 10–13.

> For as many as are of the works of the law are under the curse: for it is written, Cursed is every one that continueth not in all things which are written in the book of the law to do them. (Galatians 3:10)

In other words, those whose faith is in their own ability to keep the law are cursed. They are cursed because they will never be able to perfectly do all the commandments. And if you are counting on your own righteousness, consider that Isaiah the prophet said that all our righteousness is just filthy rags in his sight (Isaiah 64:6). Furthermore, we have all sinned and fallen short of the glory of God. If your confidence is in your own works, you will not be justified before God. The law says that whoever does not do all things written in the law is cursed.

> But that no man is justified by the law in the sight of God, it is evident: for, The just shall live by faith.
> And the law is not of faith: but, The man that doeth them shall live in them.
> Christ hath redeemed us from the curse of the law, being made a curse for us: for it is written, Cursed is every one that hangeth on a tree:

That the blessing of Abraham might
come on the Gentiles through Jesus
Christ; that we might receive the promise of the Spirit through faith. (Galatians
3:11–14)

In verse 13 it says that Christ has redeemed us from
the curse of the law. Many Christians quote that verse and
assume that now we don't keep the law anymore because
Christ redeemed us from the curse of the law. That is a mock-
ing spirit, and God is not mocked. Whatever we sow, that we
will reap. We were cursed because of sin. The law says that
the payment for our sin is death. Therefore, since we have all
sinned, we all deserve death. Christ has redeemed us from the
curse of the law.

For the wages of sin is death; but the
gift of God is eternal life through Jesus
Christ our Lord. (Romans 6:23)

Now go on to verse 16 in Galatians 3.

Now to Abraham and his seed were
the promises made. He saith not, And to
seeds, as of many; but as of one, And to
thy seed, which is Christ.
And this I say, that the covenant,
that was confirmed before of God in
Christ, the law, which was four hundred
and thirty years after, cannot disannul,
that it should make the promise of none
effect.

> For if the inheritance be of the law, it is no more of promise: but God gave it to Abraham by promise.
>
> Wherefore then serveth the law? It was added because of transgressions, till the seed should come to whom the promise was made; and it was ordained by angels in the hand of a mediator. (Galatians 3:16–19)

God gave the promises to Abraham, the father of faith, and to his seed, which is Christ. Then the law came afterward. The inheritance was given by a promise to Abraham and to his seed.

Read on starting in verse 21.

> Is the law then against the promises of God? God forbid: for if there had been a law given which could have given life, verily righteousness should have been by the law.
>
> But the scripture hath concluded all under sin, that the promise by faith of Jesus Christ might be given to them that believe.
>
> But before faith came, we were kept under the law, shut up unto the faith which should afterwards be revealed.
>
> Wherefore the law was our schoolmaster to bring us unto Christ, that we might be justified by faith. (Galatians 3:21–24)

The law was our schoolmaster to bring us to Christ. We learned earlier that we would not know we were sinners in the first place if the law was not still in place. God gave the law. But when we broke the law, we became sinners before God. Then when we were convicted of our sin, and we sought to be made right with God, that in turn led us to Christ to seek justification by faith in Him.

God made the rules. It is a sin to break God's laws. According to the law, there must be an atonement for sin (breaking the law) by the shedding of blood.

> And almost all things are by the law
> purged with blood; and without shedding
> of blood is no remission. (Hebrews 9:22)

That is why, in the past, Israel sacrificed animals, such as sheep, goats, and bulls. That is how they made atonement for sins. When Jesus came and offered His sinless life on the cross, he became the sacrifice for sins. That is how Jesus fulfilled the law.

> But after that faith is come, we are
> no longer under a schoolmaster.
> For ye are all the children of God by
> faith in Christ Jesus.
> For as many of you as have been
> baptized into Christ have put on Christ.
> There is neither Jew nor Greek,
> there is neither bond nor free, there is
> neither male nor female: for ye are all one
> in Christ Jesus.
> And if ye be Christ's, then are ye
> Abraham's seed, and heirs according to
> the promise. (Galatians 3:25–29)

Now that we have faith, we are no longer under a schoolmaster. Consider it this way: We went to school to learn things. Once the lessons were learned and the exams passed, we graduated. What did we learn from the law? We learned that we are sinners and fall short of God's glory. We learned that our own righteousness will never be good enough to save us. The law taught that there must be a sacrifice for sins. God made provision for us when he sent his Son, Jesus, to die on the cross. So to be justified in his sight, we found that we needed to be saved by God's grace by Jesus Christ.

Now that we have learned our lessons, hopefully we don't need to go back to school and learn all over again. That is what it means when we are no longer under a schoolmaster. But the facts are still true; two plus two still equals four. And that's also why Paul said we are no longer under the law. It doesn't mean that the rules are no longer in place.

Okay, by now we should be able to see that Paul was not teaching against the law. He taught us from the law. What Paul taught us is very simple, and yet it is deep. Although we have sinned, we can be made right with God. We are justified by faith not by our works. We who believe in Jesus have by faith become Abraham's seed and heirs, according to the promise. Praise God.

When a person accepts Christ as their Savior, it doesn't mean that they are will never sin again. There will always be temptations to sin for as long as we live in our bodies. We must admit that we are not perfect.

Go to the book of 1 John.

> This then is the message which we
> have heard of him, and declare unto you,
> that God is light, and in him is no dark-
> ness at all.

If we say that we have fellowship
with him, and walk in darkness, we lie,
and do not the truth:

But if we walk in the light, as he is
in the light, we have fellowship one with
another, and the blood of Jesus Christ his
Son cleanseth us from all sin.

If we say that we have no sin, we
deceive ourselves, and the truth is not in
us.

If we confess our sins, he is faithful and just to forgive us our sins, and to
cleanse us from all unrighteousness.

If we say that we have not sinned,
we make him a liar, and his word is not
in us. (1 John 1:5–10)

If we sin or break his law, we should repent and ask God
to forgive us and then go on. Fortunately, God is gracious
to forgive us when we confess our sins. However, it doesn't
mean that we won't reap what we have sown. There are still
consequences for sin. Remember what happened to King
David when he sinned in the whole affair with Bathsheba?
Although David later repented for those sins, he was still
punished, and his life was changed dramatically afterward.
(See 2 Samuel, chapters 11 and 12.)

Now consider the following words from the Apostle
Peter and notice that he was quoting the Scriptures:

But as he which hath called you is
holy, so be ye holy in all manner of conversation; Because it is written, Be ye
holy; for I am holy. (1 Peter 1:15–16)

More to be desired are they than gold,
yea, than much fine gold: sweeter also
than honey and the honeycomb.

—Psalm 19:10

Chapter 4

In Galatians, chapter 4, Paul taught more from the Scriptures and from the life of Abraham. Abraham's first son was born of Hagar, the bondwoman, while Isaac, the child of promise, was born to Abraham's wife, Sarah, who was free.

Tell me, ye that desire to be under the law, do ye not hear the law? For it is written, that Abraham had two sons, the one by a bondmaid, the other by a freewoman. But he who was of the bond-woman was born after the flesh; but he of the freewoman was by promise. Which things are an allegory: for these are the two covenants; the one from the mount Sinai, which gendereth to bondage, which is Agar. For this Agar is mount Sinai in Arabia, and answereth to Jerusalem which now is, and is in bondage with her children. But Jerusalem which is above is free, which is the mother of us all. For it is written, Rejoice, thou barren that bearest not; break forth and cry, thou that travailest not: for the desolate hath many more children than she which hath an husband. Now we, brethren, as Isaac was, are the children of promise. But as then he that was born after the flesh persecuted him that was born after the Spirit, even so it is now. Nevertheless what saith the scripture? Cast out the bondwoman and her son: for the son of the bondwoman shall not be heir with the son of the freewoman. So then, brethren, we are not children of the bondwoman, but of the free. (Galatians 4:21–31)

Paul compared the two sons of Abraham and said they were an allegory of the two covenants. According to the dictionary, an allegory can be a story that is interpreted to reveal a hidden meaning. We that have believed in God's promise of salvation through Jesus are like Isaac, the child of promise, and are born of the Spirit. Those born of the bondwoman are like those born of the flesh. Those that have put their trust in Jesus are born of the Spirit (not of the flesh).

Turn to John chapter 1.

But as many as received him, to them gave he power to become the sons of God, even to them that believe on his name:

Which were born, not of blood, nor of the will of the flesh, nor of the will of man, but of God. (John 1:12–13)

Now turn to John, chapter 3.

> Jesus answered and said unto him, Verily, verily, I say unto thee, Except a man be born again, he cannot see the kingdom of God.
>
> Nicodemus saith unto him, How can a man be born when he is old? can he enter the second time into his mother's womb, and be born?
>
> Jesus answered, Verily, verily, I say unto thee, Except a man be born of water and of the Spirit, he cannot enter into the kingdom of God.
>
> That which is born of the flesh is flesh; and that which is born of the Spirit is spirit.
>
> Marvel not that I said unto thee, Ye must be born again. (John 3:3–7)

Nicodemus asked Jesus, "How can a man be born again when he is old? He can't enter again into his mother's womb."

Jesus said we must be born of water and of the Spirit.

Now we might think we understand how a child is born. First, a man and woman come together, and a child is conceived. Then the baby is nourished in its mother's womb until it is born. But it is still a great mystery how a baby is made and formed in the womb, and it is a miracle.

The new birth that Jesus spoke about is also a mystery and a miracle. Jesus said we must be born again of water and of the Spirit to enter the kingdom of God. John said that as many as believed in him (Jesus), God gave them the power to become children of God. Some kind of miracle happens when we put our faith in Jesus Christ.

> Therefore if any man be in Christ,
> he is a new creature: old things are passed
> away; behold, all things are become new.
> (2 Corinthians 5:17 KJV)

Maybe we should stop and consider what a gift God has offered to us. When we accept the gift of salvation that Jesus offers, we can be saved from death and eternal hell. We can be forgiven of our sins. (But God also expects us to forgive those who sinned against us.) We are born again as children of God and become members of God's family, where our citizenship is in heaven. When we die, we can go to heaven to live with him throughout eternity, and Jesus promised to have a home for us there. Wow.

Now let's go on to chapter 5 in Galatians.

> Stand fast therefore in the liberty
> wherewith Christ hath made us free, and
> be not entangled again with the yoke of
> bondage. (Galatians 5:1)

Once again, with the old mindset, Christians took this verse out of context. We assumed that it meant that we have liberty now, and if we start keeping the law, it will lead us into bondage. What was Paul talking about? It is the same thing he had been teaching from the beginning.

In the first place, Paul had just finished talking about the difference between the children of the bondwoman (Hagar) and children of the free woman (Sarah). There was probably not a chapter break here in Paul's letter to the Galatians. Let's go to the last verse of chapter 4 and then continue reading the next verse.

> So then, brethren, we are not children of the bondwoman, but of the free.
> Stand fast therefore in the liberty wherewith Christ hath made us free, and be not entangled again with the yoke of bondage.

Stand fast in the liberty, wherewith Christ made us free. Who made us free? Christ did.

> Then said Jesus to those Jews which believed on him, If ye continue in my word, then are ye my disciples indeed;
> And ye shall know the truth, and the truth shall make you free.
> They answered him, We be Abraham's seed, and were never in bondage to any man: how sayest thou, Ye shall be made free?
> Jesus answered them, Verily, verily, I say unto you, Whosoever committeth sin is the servant of sin.
> And the servant abideth not in the house for ever: but the Son abideth ever.
> If the Son therefore shall make you free, ye shall be free indeed. (John 8:31–36)

Jesus told the Jews that if they continued in his word, they would be his disciples. They would know the truth, and the truth would make them free. What is the truth?—whoever sins becomes a slave to sin (verse 34 above). What is sin? Sin is breaking the law of God.

> Whosoever committeth sin transgresseth also the law: for sin is the transgression of the law. (1 John 3:4)

We all have sinned. When we sinned, we became servants to sin. Jesus said that if the Son makes you free, you shall be free indeed.

Now let's read 1 John 3:4–10 in the English Standard Version.

> Everyone who makes a practice of sinning also practices lawlessness; sin is lawlessness. You know that he appeared in order to take away sins, and in him there is no sin. No one who abides in him keeps on sinning; no one who keeps on sinning has either seen him or known him. Little children, let no one deceive you. Whoever practices righteousness is righteous, as he is righteous. Whoever makes a practice of sinning is of the devil, for the devil has been sinning from the beginning. The reason the Son of God appeared was to destroy the works of the devil. No one born of God makes a practice of sinning, for God's seed abides in him; and he cannot keep on sinning, because he has been born of God. By this it is evident who are the children of God, and who are the children of the devil: whoever does not practice righteousness

is not of God, nor is the one who does not love his brother.

Go to Romans 6:1–23.

> What shall we say then? Shall we continue in sin, that grace may abound? (verse 1)

Shall we keep on sinning? Just because we have Jesus as our Savior doesn't mean that we can do whatever we want to. God gave us rules to follow, and those are his commandments. When we break his rules, we sin.

Go down to verse 8 in Romans 6.

> Now if we be dead with Christ, we believe that we shall also live with him:
>
> Knowing that Christ being raised from the dead dieth no more; death hath no more dominion over him.
>
> For in that he died, he died unto sin once: but in that he liveth, he liveth unto God.
>
> Likewise reckon ye also yourselves to be dead indeed unto sin, but alive unto God through Jesus Christ our Lord.
>
> Let not sin therefore reign in your mortal body, that ye should obey it in the lusts thereof.
>
> Neither yield ye your members as instruments of unrighteousness unto sin: but yield yourselves unto God, as those that are alive from the dead, and your

members as instruments of righteousness unto God.

For sin shall not have dominion over you: for ye are not under the law, but under grace.

What then? shall we sin, because we are not under the law, but under grace? God forbid.

Know ye not, that to whom ye yield yourselves servants to obey, his servants ye are to whom ye obey; whether of sin unto death, or of obedience unto righteousness?

But God be thanked, that ye were the servants of sin, but ye have obeyed from the heart that form of doctrine which was delivered you.

Being then made free from sin, ye became the servants of righteousness…

For when ye were the servants of sin, ye were free from righteousness.

What fruit had ye then in those things whereof ye are now ashamed? for the end of those things is death.

But now being made free from sin, and become servants to God, ye have your fruit unto holiness, and the end everlasting life.

For the wages of sin is death; but the gift of God is eternal life through Jesus Christ our Lord. (verses 8–18, 20–23)

Look at verses 14 through 16 again. Sin shall not have dominion or rule over you.

> For sin shall not have dominion over you: for ye are not under the law, but under grace.
>
> What then? shall we sin, because we are not under the law, but under grace? God forbid.
>
> Know ye not, that to whom ye yield yourselves servants to obey, his servants ye are to whom ye obey; whether of sin unto death, or of obedience unto righteousness?

Now we can see that when Paul said we are not under the law but under grace, he did not mean we don't keep the commandments. When we broke the law, we sinned and became servants (slaves) of sin. But when we believed the doctrine (put our faith in Jesus), we were made free from serving sin and became servants of righteousness (verses 17–18 above). Jesus came to save us and to set us free from our bondage to sin. Keeping the law does not bring us into bondage. (But when we get legalistic about it, like the Pharisees, that can lead us into bondage as well.)

See Romans 6:23.

> For the wages of sin is death; but the gift of God is eternal life through Jesus Christ our Lord.

Praise God. We all have sinned, and we all deserve death. We deserve death, yet God, in his mercy, gave us the gift of eternal life through Jesus Christ. We don't deserve it, and we can't earn it. Do we keep the law so that we can be saved? We have all sinned and deserve death. We can't earn our salvation. Salvation is a gift. We are saved by grace through faith.

> For God so loved the world, that he gave his only begotten Son, that whosoever believeth in him should not perish, but have everlasting life. (John 3:16)

Can we earn God's love? God's love came without conditions. God loves us just as we are, but that doesn't mean he wants us to stay that way. If we are living in sin, our lives can be a mess. But we can simply accept His love and mercy and repent and turn away from our sins and then simply receive the gift that God is offering to us through Jesus Christ. Then we keep the law because God said to do those things. And those that love God keep his commandments.

> But showing mercy to thousands, to those who love Me and keep My commandments. (Exodus 20:6)

> And I prayed to the Lord my God, and made confession, and said, "O Lord, great and awesome God, who keeps His covenant and mercy with those who love Him, and with those who keep His commandments." (Daniel 9:4)

> He who has My commandments and keeps them, it is he who loves Me. And he who loves Me will be loved by My Father, and I will love him and manifest Myself to him. (John 15:21)

Now let's go back again and read the first verses in Galatians, chapter 5.

> Stand fast therefore in the liberty wherewith Christ hath made us free, and be not entangled again with the yoke of bondage.
>
> Behold, I Paul say unto you, that if ye be circumcised, Christ shall profit you nothing.
>
> For I testify again to every man that is circumcised, that he is a debtor to do the whole law.
>
> Christ is become of no effect unto you, whosoever of you are justified by the law; ye are fallen from grace. (Galatians 5:1–4)

Look at verses 3 and 4 this way. Every man who puts his confidence in the fact that he is circumcised must keep all the law to be perfect. That's what he meant by "he is a debtor to do the whole law." Christ is of no value to you since you are counting on your own works in keeping the law. You have fallen from grace.

Okay, now let's go back to the beginning and look again at what happened when Paul and the others went up to Jerusalem. Remember the reason that they didn't give in to pressure and have Titus circumcised? Go back to Galatians, chapter 2.

> And that because of false brethren unawares brought in, who came in privily to spy out our liberty which we have in Christ Jesus, that they might bring us into bondage:

> To whom we gave place by subjec-
> tion, no, not for an hour; that the truth
> of the gospel might continue with you.
> (Galatians 2:4–5 KJV)

Paul took a stand to preserve the truth of the gospel. False brethren had crept into the church to secretly spy out the *liberty* that they had in Christ Jesus. Certain Pharisees wanted to bring them into *bondage* by adding legalist requirements, such as circumcision, before men could be saved.

Did you notice the words *liberty* and *bondage* above in those verses? And that is what happens when you put your confidence in your own abilities to do all the law. You will always be striving, and you will never be good enough. The truth of the gospel is that we are saved by grace through faith in Jesus Christ.

Go to Romans, chapter 10. Look at verses 9–13.

> That if thou shalt confess with thy
> mouth the Lord Jesus, and shalt believe
> in thine heart that God hath raised him
> from the dead, thou shalt be saved.
> For with the heart man believeth
> unto righteousness; and with the mouth
> confession is made unto salvation.
> For the scripture saith, Whosoever
> believeth on him shall not be ashamed.
> For there is no difference between
> the Jew and the Greek: for the same Lord
> over all is rich unto all that call upon him.
> For whosoever shall call upon the
> name of the Lord shall be saved. (Romans
> 10:9–13)

Okay, now it should be easier to see what the Apostle Paul was talking about. Somehow, the church got it all mixed up, and people pointed to the book of Galatians and said, "Now we don't need to keep the law." It is exactly like what the Apostle Peter said about Paul being misunderstood.

> And account that the longsuffering of our Lord is salvation; even as our beloved brother Paul also according to the wisdom given unto him hath written unto you;
>
> As also in all his epistles, speaking in them of these things; in which are some things hard to be understood, which they that are unlearned and unstable wrest, as they do also the other scriptures, unto their own destruction. (2 Peter 3:15–16)

Moreover by them is thy servant
warned: and in keeping of
them there is great reward.

—Psalm 19:11 KJV

Conclusion

Okay, now we have looked at the book of Galatians from another viewpoint, and hopefully we have understood the teachings of the Apostle Paul with a new mindset. Paul was not teaching against circumcision or the law. Instead, he was laying the foundation of our faith that we are saved by grace through faith in Jesus Christ. And that is the truth of the gospel.

Now that we have seen the book of Galatians in a different light, let's look at some other verses in the New Testament and see if we can understand them with a new mindset. Turn to the first book of Corinthians 7:18.

Is any man called being circumcised? let him not become uncircumcised. Is any called in uncircumcision? let him not be circumcised.

Circumcision is nothing, and uncircumcision is nothing, but the keeping of the commandments of God.

Let every man abide in the same calling wherein he was called.

Art thou called being a servant? care
not for it: but if thou mayest be made free,
use it rather. (1 Corinthians 7:18–21)

Christians that are of the mindset that Paul was against circumcision or the law might see these verses to mean that circumcision is not important at all. However, when we understand that the Apostle Paul kept the law and did not preach against it, we can begin to see what he meant.

In the first place, Paul was not talking about men getting circumcised or uncircumcised. How does a man get uncircumcised anyway? Look at it this way: The Jews were called the circumcision group, and the Gentiles were called the uncircumcision group. Paul was saying that if you were a Jew when you were called, then you don't have to become a Gentile. If you were a Gentile when you were called, then you don't have to become a Jew. Were you a servant or slave when you were called? If you can obtain your freedom, go ahead. What Paul was saying in essence is that you can serve the Lord in whatever status you were when you were called.

Now, in verse 19, Paul said circumcision is nothing, and uncircumcision is nothing but the keeping of the commandments of God. Here again, he is not talking against circumcision. He was saying that circumcision is just keeping the commandments. Duh. Paul was only trying to say that it didn't matter if you were a Jew or a Gentile when you were called.

Now let's look at other verses that many Christians have taken out of context. Consider the vision that the Apostle Peter had, as we mentioned in Acts, chapter 10. Peter had a vision of all manner of unclean foods, and he was told to get up, kill, and eat. Since Peter was a Jew, he understood the dietary rules and told the Lord that he never ate anything unclean. The Lord answered Peter and said that he should not call unclean what God had cleansed.

Now Christians have used this story to support their wrong mindset. Some people have misunderstood the reason for the vision. Some have said that Peter was given the vision to show that all kinds of food have been cleansed, so now we can eat whatever we want. Of course, we have free will to eat whatever we want to eat, but that doesn't mean it's good for you. And that was *not* why Peter was given the vision of the unclean animals. It is a good thing that Peter didn't interpret the vision that way. Peter understood the meaning of the vision. The vision was given to Peter to show him that God purified the hearts of the Gentiles by faith and that Peter, as a Jew, was not to call them unclean. (The Jews considered the Gentiles to be unclean.)

Now let's look at the time when Jesus told his disciples that what defiles a man is not what he puts into his mouth but what comes out of his mouth. The Pharisees were accusing Jesus's disciples of breaking the traditions of the elders by eating with unwashed hands. Jesus explained that eating with unwashed hands doesn't defile a man. But what a man says or what comes out of his mouth is what defiles a person. Jesus went on to explain that what comes out of the mouth—things like evil thoughts, murder, adultery, and fornication, which come from a man's heart—is what defiles a man, not what a man puts into his mouth. (See Matthew 15 and Mark 7.)

People have taken that story out of context and tried to say that it means we can eat whatever foods we want. They have taken the lesson out of context to support their own mindset and disregard the dietary rules found in the Torah. Jesus never spoke against the law. In the first place, they were not talking about food defiling a person but about eating with unwashed hands. Jesus said, that doesn't defile you, but what defiles a man is what comes out of the heart. Jesus was not giving a lesson on dietary instructions.

> And he saith unto them, Are ye so without understanding also? Do ye not perceive, that whatsoever thing from without entereth into the man, it cannot defile him;
> Because it entereth not into his heart, but into the belly, and goeth out into the draught, purging all meats?
> And he said, That which cometh out of the man, that defileth the man.
> For from within, out of the heart of men, proceed evil thoughts, adulteries, fornications, murders,
> Thefts, covetousness, wickedness, deceit, lasciviousness, an evil eye, blasphemy, pride, foolishness:
> All these evil things come from within, and defile the man. (Mark 7:18–23)

Please note: There are even some modern manuscripts that add a sentence to Mark 7:19 to support this hypocrisy. Notice what has been added to verse 19 in some modern translations. The words following in parenthesis were not in the original manuscripts.

> Since it enters not his heart but his stomach, and is expelled? (Thus he declared all foods clean.) (ESV)

Okay, now let's go look at another verse in the New Testament and see if we can see it with a new mindset. Go to the book of Hebrews, and read chapters 3 and 4. Consider the following verse:

> There remains, then, a Sabbath-
> rest for the people of God. (Hebrews 4:9
> NIV)

It says there remains a Sabbath rest for the people of God. Some people argue that Jesus is our rest, so we don't need to keep the Sabbath anymore. That is the old mindset.

Instead, let's consider it this way. There remains a Sabbath rest for the people of God. God rested from all His works on the seventh day. When we put our trust in Jesus and his finished work on the cross, we can rest from striving to obtain salvation by our own works. We accept His grace. Then we rest in the fact that we are saved by grace.

> Therefore being justified by faith,
> we have peace with God through our
> Lord Jesus Christ. (Romans 5:1)

Now we understand that we can have peace with God because of what Jesus has done. Let us strive to enter that rest. But that doesn't replace the commandment to keep the Sabbath. The Sabbath is the seventh day when God rested from His work. God set that day apart and sanctified it, making it holy. Now we should rest from our work on that day because God said to remember the Sabbath and keep it holy. That is how we honor and serve God, by doing what He says.

God's word is true. Just because we didn't understand things did not mean it was okay to disregard certain commandments. In the past, God winked at some of those things, but now, God is giving revelation to His servants, and with that revelation comes more understanding. And having understanding brings more responsibility. It's like growing up.

Furthermore, there are blessings for obeying God and keeping His words or commandments, and there are curses for not keeping them. The blessings and curses are found in Deuteronomy 28. It is written in the word of God, and God doesn't change. If we lie, steal, and commit adultery or any other sins, do we think we will be blessed for doing those things? Jesus said He came that we might have life and have it abundantly. However, Jesus also said that the enemy came to steal, kill, and destroy. If anyone feels they are getting ripped off, then maybe they should stop doing those things that are sins and start listening to Jesus and do those things that are right.

Are we still unsure? God gave us a way to prove Him—by bringing in our tithes. Prove me in this. Many sermons have been preached about tithing, and God's promises are still true. There are testimonies from people who have taken God at His word and have put God to the test and paid their tithes and have been blessed, financially and otherwise.

There are blessings as well for keeping the Sabbath and the other commandments in the Bible. If we honor our father and mother, God said, things will go well for us. But if we show our parents dishonor, that is not pleasing to God, and there will be consequences. If we are obedient to His word, we will be blessed. There are blessings for obedience and curses for disobedience. And who doesn't want to be blessed more and more?

God gave his Son and made provision for our sins. Salvation is a great gift! It is the greatest gift of all because we are promised eternal life. Salvation, however, is only the beginning. There are more promises in God's word. Peter said that we have been given exceedingly great and precious promises (2 Peter 1:4).

As Christians, we are born again when we accept Jesus as our Savior. However, it is sad that many Christians want to remain as babies. They don't want to grow up and become responsible for themselves. They don't read the Bible for themselves because they want others to feed them and take care of them. Consider what the Apostle Peter said.

> As newborn babes, desire the sincere milk of the word, that ye may grow thereby: If so be ye have tasted that the Lord is gracious. (1 Peter 2:2–3)

Newborn babies are very hungry for their milk. Their very survival depends upon getting that nourishment. And Christians should be very hungry for the Word of God. The trouble has been that the Word has been watered down by preachers that don't want to offend. And there's also been a lack of understanding of what it means to be a Christian. We have taken parts of the Bible to be true, while other parts of Scriptures have been put aside because we didn't understand what it meant.

However, in these last days, God is bringing forth knowledge and a better understanding of the Bible and what it means to serve this living God. And as people are beginning to wake up and see what is going on in the world, they are becoming hungry for the truth. Hopefully, God's people will begin to mature as they desire the sincere milk of the Word because our very survival may depend upon it.

Okay, finally, in conclusion, we have looked at the book of Galatians and have begun to see how the Apostle Paul has been misunderstood. Most of us have been looking at Paul and his writings through the wrong mindset. Somehow, the doctrine has crept into the churches that Paul was teaching against the law.

Once again, the Apostle Peter said that Paul was so learned that ignorant and unstable men would come and twist the scriptures. Who was ignorant? We Gentiles were ignorant when it came to the Scriptures. Jesus came to fulfill the law, not to destroy it. God will never go back on His word. You should read the whole Bible and not just the New Testament. God doesn't change, and neither does Jesus. And Jesus is one with the Father. When Jesus came, the message that he preached was, "Repent, for the kingdom of God is at hand." And Jesus Christ is the same yesterday, today, and forever.

The law of the Lᴏʀᴅ is perfect, converting the soul: the testimony of the Lᴏʀᴅ is sure, making wise the simple.

The statutes of the Lᴏʀᴅ are right, rejoicing the heart: the commandment of the Lᴏʀᴅ is pure, enlightening the eyes.

The fear of the Lᴏʀᴅ is clean, enduring for ever: the judgments of the Lᴏʀᴅ are true and righteous altogether.

More to be desired are they than gold, yea, than much fine gold: sweeter also than honey and the honeycomb.

Moreover by them is thy servant warned: and in keeping of them there is great reward. (Psalm 19:7–11 KJV)

Therefore I love thy commandments above gold; yea, above fine gold. (Psalm 119:127)

Afterword

There is a mystery that has been hidden in the scriptures for centuries. However, in recent times it has been revealed.

> Ephraim, he hath mixed himself among the people; Ephraim is a cake not turned. (Hosea 7:8)

Who is Ephraim? Manasseh and Ephraim were the two sons of Joseph that were born to him in Egypt. When Joseph brought his sons to his father Jacob to be blessed by him, Jacob stretched forth his hands to bless them. Jacob put his right hand on Ephraim and said that he would become the fulness of the Gentiles.

Ephraim is the house of Israel. After King Solomon died, the kingdom of Israel was divided into two houses. The ten tribes of the northern kingdom were known as the house of Israel or Ephraim. The two tribes that stayed in Jerusalem were called the house of Judah. The house of Judah consisted of the tribes of Judah and Benjamin and included the Levites. They were known as the Jews, and they kept their identity to the God of their fathers.

However, the house of Israel rebelled against God, and the northern kingdom was conquered by the king of Assyria and carried away into captivity in 722 BC. Those ten tribes lost their identity when they were scattered among the nations. They became known as the lost sheep of the house of Israel.

When Jesus came, he told his disciples that he came only for the lost sheep of the house of Israel (Matthew 15:24). When Jesus sent his disciples out to preach, he told them to go to the lost sheep of the house of Israel. Furthermore, Jesus told us that the son of man came to seek and to save that which was lost (Luke 19:10).

Ephraim, for the most part, are the Christians, those that were drawn to the Messiah. And according to a modern-day Jewish prophet, when Hosea said that Ephraim is a cake not turned, that meant that Ephraim (the church) has the Messiah but does not have the law. They are like a pancake that is cooked only on one side.